Take The F***ing Fly

Fly fishing wisdoms & frustrations—an irreverent poem

by Milt Mays
illustrated by Mike Friehauf

All rights reserved. This book, or parts thereof, may not be reproduced in any form without permission from the author and/or artist. No part of this text may be reproduced, transmitted, downloaded, decompiled, reverse engineered, or stored in or introduced into any information storage and retrieval system, in any form or by any means, whether electronic or mechanical without the express written permission of the author. The scanning, uploading and distribution of this book via the Internet or via any other means without the permission of the publisher is illegal and punishable by law. Please purchase only authorized, and do not participate in or encourage piracy of copyrighted materials.

If you purchased this book without a cover, you should be aware that this book is stolen property. It was reported as "unsold and destroyed" by the publisher and neither the author nor the publisher has received any payment for this "stripped book."

Discover more by this author at www.MiltMays.com and the artist at StoneflyGraphics.com.

Words ©2013 Milt Mays • MiltMays.com

Illustrations ©2013 Mike Friehauf • StoneflyGraphics.com

ISBN-13: 978-0-9913297-9-3

Dedicated to the Bighorn River,
our Bighorn fishing partners &
anyone who has ever had *The Funk*.

Mood descends, slow, but sure.
I know they're there —
Scott and Mike caught four,
Ken had a pair,
But not me.
Please fish, take the f*king fly.

The River still runs,
The hawk still screams,
Snow-capped mountains ask me to be free.
I won't hear,
Can't see
Because the fish are ignoring my fking fly.

THE FUNK cloaks my heart,
Hazes my mind,
Chokes out fun,
Good friends, and sunshine.

All for a fish

That will eat that f*cking fly.

Don't need a BIG fish,
A hundred, or twenty.
One would be plenty.
Maybe five or six-ish.
Cast, drift, mend.
Nothing.
The fish hate my f*cking fly.

I'm just not as good at fishing as they.
Can't get it done today.
Same hole, same depth, same fly,
Same, same, same.
Or so it seems.

Change that mindset.
Think—It WILL!
It's coming, for sure
It's coming.
It doesn't.
F*ck this shit.

Change your lips,
Hold your mouth different.
Cast, drift, mend.
Come on!
Nothing.
Time to break the f*cking rod.

Move up a little, right there, yeah
Where that other guy is casting.
Oh look, he caught another.
I got nothing.

What am I doing wrong?
Bad juju must be it.
The hat? The gloves? The shitbird fly?
Change that fly, change it again.
Make it deeper, different color.
Yes, that's gotta be it.
Cast, drift, mend.
Gotta be there, gotta be there…
Nothing.
Fuck.

They are laughing.
He got a big fish,
She got four,
He got five,
I got none.
That's me.
The f*ckhead who can't fish.

THE FUNK sucks me dry.
No talking, sulky quiet.
But it talks to me,
You're a BAAAD fisherman, face it.
You can't catch fish. Just the way it is.
Take a deep breath
Look around,
Enjoy the f*cking view.
Cast, drift, mend.
Yeah, of course.
Nothing.
No big deal.
It's only f*cking fishing.

ARE YOU KIDDING ME?
A pull and wiggle is all I want.

Not much to ask.

Say a prayer, ask it nice.

Come on God, *please*.

Cast, drift…Yes!

That is it!

No, just bottom.

F##k the nice talk.

This sucks.

Night falls, sleep calls.
Wake up early, toss and turn.
What can I do?
Change the leader, tippet, fly,
You f***ing stupid poo.
Bad juju out.
Good juju in.
Try again you dope.

Take my time, cast it out.
Catch the first one, wiggle heaven.
Could THE FUNK be gone?
Catch a second and another.
The River chuckles.
The hawk cheers.
Those mountains are gorgeous.
Now I see
Now I hear.
This is f*ckliscious!

Ken goes fishless in that hole.
Glancing up I see his eyes,
His stare is covered with a haze.
THE FUNK has climbed into his brain.
I comfort him and pat his back,
And drop down further,
Catch another.
Holy F*ck!

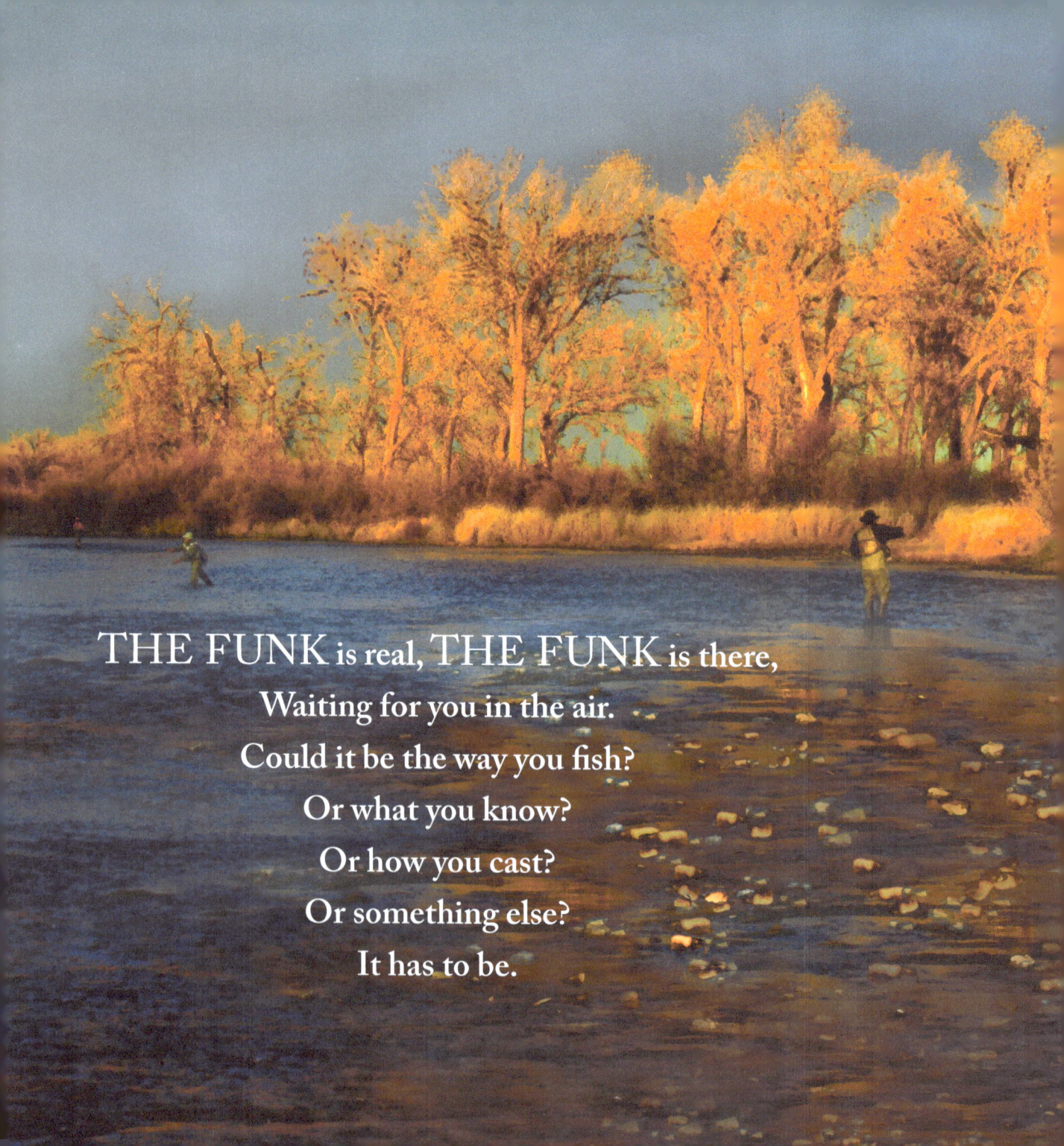

THE FUNK is real, THE FUNK is there,
Waiting for you in the air.
Could it be the way you fish?
Or what you know?
Or how you cast?
Or something else?
It has to be.

I think it more a state of mind,
Or maybe luck,
Or you're just f*cked.
Could be a virus.
Whatever it is, Ken's got it now.

The End

Other published works by Milt Mays include a novel, Dan's War, short stories, "Thanksgiving with Riley" and "The Dry-Land Farmer." Milt has been a guide on the Big Thompson River and in Rocky Mountain National Park in Northern Colorado. His new novel is *The Guide*, A backcountry trip gone sour in Rocky Mountain National Park. A serial killer…a doctor…and the guide who stands between them. All his works are available on Amazon, or go to www.miltmays.com.

Mike Friehauf has worked as a graphic designer, art director, & illustrator in the tech industry for 20 plus years and has been waiting patiently for an opportunity to illustrate a book having to do with his greatest passion — *fly fishing*.

A special thanks to the Bighorn Gang for their comic inspiration as well as photos used to create these illustrations & in particular to Ken Eis & Scott Lazarowicz who provided some of the more dramatic photos used for the artwork in this book.

A huge thanks to Scott for his years of unselfishly organizing our trips to the Bighorn River, and showing us the beauty and fun of fly fishing.
—MM & MF

www.ingramcontent.com/pod-product-compliance
Lightning Source LLC
Chambersburg PA
CBHW041934160426
42813CB00103B/2919